Beautifully
BRAVE

60 days for

CWR

Contents

'What to be?' That's the question!

'Be popular ... Be smart ... Be funny ... Be pretty ... Be the best ... Be ... Be ... Be!'

When you start following God, you begin to realise – more and more – that these things aren't actually as important as people try to make out! And being these things doesn't actually make us as happy as they seem to promise. That's because God created us for so much more than this!

He has great adventures in store for us; good, exciting plans that will take us in directions we never imagined! And as we follow His path for our lives, as we grow in our faith, opportunities will pop up along the way. These might be anything from telling another friend about Jesus, standing up for what we believe in front of a group of people or even going to another country to help a Christian charity!

In all these things, we need to exercise a certain something – bravery!

Stepping out of our comfort zones can be as hard as jumping out of a plane! But let's not allow fear to hold us back from such an exhilarating experience!

There are loads of examples in the Bible of people, totally ordinary people, doing the most extraordinary things because they trusted God and stepped out in faith. As you get to know God more, and as you put your life into His hands, *you* can follow in their brave footsteps!

So read on! Here's what we're going to explore …

First up, before we go 'jumping out of planes', we need to be well prepared! In **Bring it On**, we look at the passage from Ephesians on the armour of God, and find out what each piece of armour represents and how it will help protect and prepare us for whatever life throws at us!

Then we think about what it means to be **Deliberately Different**. Based on Jesus' Sermon on the Mount, this section is about ways of bravely living as Jesus taught, which often goes against the flow of those around us.

Powered by Praise is all about how worshipping God – thanking Him and focusing on Him – can give us the boost we need to live courageously.

Finally, we look at **Sisterhood**. We'll explore some great examples of brave women in the Bible and think about how we can encourage, support and help each other as women of God.

We hope you enjoy this book and that it will help you to **live the life God planned for you by being completely, beautifully brave!**

'be strong in the Lord and in his mighty power. Put on the full armour of God, so that you can take your stand against the devil's schemes. For our struggle is not against flesh and blood, but against the rulers, against the authorities, against the powers of this dark world and against the spiritual forces of evil in the heavenly realms. Therefore put on the full armour of God, so that when the day of evil comes, you may be able to stand your ground, and after you have done everything, to stand.' **Ephesians 6:10–13**

Struggle?

Powers? Armour? Has this got anything to do with *me*? You may very well be asking these questions! The truth is **there is a fight going on,** not between each of us, but between good and evil, and whether we know it or not, it affects us all.

When you decide to follow Jesus, you are making the best decision of your life! You become a child of God (just like that!) and inherit all the benefits: purpose for your life, love and guidance from God, the Holy Spirit and, let's not forget, the promise of an eternity spent in heaven! Amazing!

When you become a Christian you have the greatest hope for your future. BUT, right here and right now, you might not experience the easiest or most perfect life on earth. Why? Because God has an enemy, Satan (aka the devil), whose ultimate goal is to keep us from following God.

Let's find out exactly how the devil works so that we can be wise and keep God at the centre! God has not left us alone in this – no way! Paul, the writer of Ephesians, tells us about the armour of God. It will not only protect us but will help us fight back. Let's find out how!

 Read Ephesians 6:10–18 to hear the full list of the armour of God. Why not start to keep a journal of what you learn over this chapter? We're going to look at each piece of armour in turn, finding out how the devil attacks and how this armour protects and empowers us!

Dear God, thank You for Your loving protection and care. Show me how to use Your armour so that I'm prepared for anything! Amen.

I'm not going to fall for that!

'I am the LORD, and there is no other … I, the LORD, speak the truth; I declare what is right … Turn to me and be saved, all you ends of the earth; for I am God, and there is no other.' **Isaiah 45:18–19,22**

One massive difference between God and the devil – good and evil – is that God only speaks the truth and the devil loves to tell a lie or two. He whispers lies into our ears and if we're not careful we begin to believe that they're true …

'No one loves you.'

'You're ugly.'

'You're useless.'

What a load of rubbish! But it's all too easy to believe his lies from time to time, isn't it? We can't fight them off on our own – and God never intended us to. You see, God *is* truth. He never has and never will deceive us. He cannot lie. Truth is such an important part of God that He named it as His first piece of armour. 'Stand firm then, with the belt of truth buckled round your waist' (Eph. 6:14).

The Bible is FULL of God's truth. So here's an example of how we could fight the lies we read above with the truth:

God says, 'you are mine … you are precious … I love you' (Isa. 43:1,4).

You are 'fearfully and wonderfully made; [God's] works are wonderful' (Psa. 139:14).

God says, 'I know the plans I have for you … plans to prosper you and … give you hope and a future' (Jer. 29:11).

You are loved, you are beautiful and you have a purpose! This is just the start of the great truth you can find in the Bible! Makes you want to get reading, doesn't it?!

Are you feeling a bit low, or do you know someone who is down at the moment? Try to get to the root of the feeling. You'll often find a lie has snuck in: 'God doesn't care.' 'God is punishing me.' 'I'm not good enough.' It's all lies! Put on the belt of truth today. In other words, ask God to show you the truth!

Dear God, thank You that I can trust You completely. Please help me not to fall for any lies today. And equip me to help others too. Amen.

No word of a lie

'That, however, is not the way of life you learned when you heard about Christ and were taught in him in accordance with the truth that is in Jesus. You were taught, with regard to your former way of life, to put off your old self, which is being corrupted by its deceitful desires; to be made new in the attitude of your minds; and to put on the new self, created to be like God in true righteousness and holiness. Therefore each of you must put off falsehood and speak truthfully to your neighbour, for we are all members of one body.' **Ephesians 4:20–25**

God is truth. As we saw in our last reading, He is completely genuine and 100 per cent trustworthy. So, what does that make us as daughters of God? Daughters of truth, of course! Putting on the belt of truth is more than just knowing the truth, it's acting on it ourselves. Every day we have hundreds of opportunities to be truthful.

'Where's your homework?'

'What are you doing this Sunday?'

Little white lies, bending the truth, withholding information – it's tempting, isn't it? That's because the devil's tactics include persuading us that lies are the 'easy way out' of anything. But that's not who we were created to be. Today's verses encourage us to 'put off falsehood'. Did you know that people look to you, knowing you are a Christian, to see **what makes you different?** If we are just as untrustworthy as the next person, we're not being the best examples of Jesus!

We might fear the consequences of telling the truth. We might get a detention for admitting we didn't do our homework. We might get a funny look for saying we're going to church on Sunday.

These things aren't nice but they don't last. When we tell the truth, what does last is this: people will respect and trust us. They will notice that we are different, and when they ask **'Why?'** we can tell them about Jesus!

 Think about a time in the past when you told a little white lie. If you had told the truth instead, what might have been the short-term consequences (getting told off or laughed at)? Compare them to what the long-term positive outcomes may have been (being trusted or bringing someone to know Jesus).

Lord, please give me courage today to tell the truth. I want to be an example of You, the God of truth. Amen.

Brave heart

'if anyone is in Christ, the new creation has come: the old has gone, the new is here! All this is from God, who reconciled us to himself through Christ … not counting people's sins against them … We are therefore Christ's ambassadors … God made him who had no sin to be sin for us, so that in him we might become the righteousness of God.'

2 Corinthians 5:17–21

Do you ever feel you aren't quite 'good enough'? Or downhearted because you didn't do something as well as you wanted to? Guess what? This is another tactic of the devil, used to try to pull you away from God. Many people avoid church because they think it's only for 'perfect' people. They, just like ourselves, can believe that we have to *earn* God's love and approval.

The amazing and simply fantastic news is that when we believe and accept Jesus into our hearts, **God looks at us and sees Jesus.** That's part of what it means in the Bible when it says we are 'in Christ'! When Jesus went to die on the cross, He took the sin of the world, including ours, and took the punishment for it. Jesus makes us 100 percent good enough!

And that's what this big word 'righteousness' means in our second piece of armour: 'the breastplate of righteousness' (Eph. 6:14). We are 'right with God' because of Jesus!

So why a breastplate? Well, Paul, who wrote Ephesians and today's verses, knew his readers would be familiar with Roman armour, and so would have an understanding of what all the different pieces were good for. A Roman breastplate, which covered the chest, protected the soldier's vital organs. So Paul was stressing how *vitally* important righteousness is!

When the devil goes for your heart, you can remind him that your mistakes or times of falling short of perfection do not make you any less loved by God! You are right with God, perfect in His sight.

Engage

What would you say to someone who thought they were not 'good enough' or had done too many sinful things for God to be able to love them? Why not write your answer down so that you can be prepared if ever asked?

Pray

Jesus, thank You so much for wiping my slate clean so that I could be perfect in God's sight! What an amazing gift. Help me not to take it for granted and keep my heart protected. Amen.

New shoes

'Open the gates that the righteous nation may enter, the nation that keeps faith. You will keep in perfect peace those whose minds are steadfast, because they trust in you. Trust in the LORD for ever, for the LORD, the LORD himself, is the Rock eternal ... The path of the righteous is level; you, the Upright One, make the way of the righteous smooth.' **Isaiah 26:2–4,7**

Life is full of uncertainties. What will I do when I finish school? Does my family have enough money? Will my sick friend get better? It can all make us feel very anxious and uneasy. And – you guessed it – the devil wants to use our worries to pull us further and further away from the One who can actually help us. He tells us to doubt God, to cut our losses and follow him instead.

That's why we need the next piece of armour in our lives. We need to get our 'feet fitted with the readiness that comes from the gospel of peace' (Eph. 6:15). We need to put on the shoes of peace!

First though, what really is peace? Is it lying on a sun lounger? Is it times of quiet? Well, those kinds of 'peace' are all about your surroundings and circumstances.

Whereas, this real and 'perfect' peace, spoken about in today's verses, can be felt even in the worst situations. When we put our faith in God and trust He will work some good out of these bad times, we will be able to feel God's perfect peace in our hearts.

The picture of putting this peace on our feet is beautiful. **God's peace will guide us down the right path.**

Trusting in God is a leap of faith sometimes. But remember, God doesn't lie. If He says He will keep those who trust Him in perfect peace then He will!

Engage God can flatten obstacles and fill in the gaps that make us uneasy about the future. But are you heading down the path where God is smoothing out the way? Are you trusting Him today?

Pray

Father, when life is great I will trust You and when life is not easy I will still trust You. Thank You for Your care, protection and peace. I love You, God. Amen.

Watch me run!

'Therefore, since we are surrounded by such a great cloud of witnesses, let us throw off everything that hinders and the sin that so easily entangles. And let us run with perseverance the race marked out for us, fixing our eyes on Jesus, the pioneer and perfecter of faith. For the joy that was set before him he endured the cross, scorning its shame, and sat down at the right hand of the throne of God. Consider him who endured such opposition from sinners, so that you will not grow weary and lose heart.'

Hebrews 12:1–3

You can't run as fast in heels as you can in trainers. And in the same way, we can't 'run the race' of life without the right 'footwear'. Let's think a little more about the shoes of peace and compare them to the things that 'hinder' us.

When we make mistakes, when we sin, it can feel a bit like falling on your face! It not only hurts you, but also makes you feel like everyone is watching! The devil will throw anything at us to make us stumble. This might be anything from a wrong group of friends to a pushy boyfriend. He wants us to feel discouraged, angry even, so that we're less likely to go on living for God and telling others about Jesus.

So let's wise up to this and see how the shoes of peace will help us 'trample' over the devil's schemes. God's peace is uplifting; with it **we can live free,** with our eyes focused on Him. He'll sort the obstacles out (He's promised to!), we just need to keep obeying and following His way for our life.

Engage

Are you feeling weary or downhearted right now? Or do you know someone who is? Pray the following prayer for yourself or on behalf of that person. Remember, Jesus understands you completely. He experienced the greatest pain (going to the cross) but now He enjoys the greatest prize (a place at the right hand of God).

Pray

God, please pick me up, dust me off and show me the way forward. Fill me now with Your peace but also with Your joy, so that I can live for You. Thank You. Amen.

Blocked

'Be alert and of sober mind. Your enemy the devil prowls around like a roaring lion looking for someone to devour. Resist him, standing firm in the faith, because you know that the family of believers throughout the world is undergoing the same kind of sufferings. And the God of all grace, who called you to his eternal glory in Christ, after you have suffered a little while, will himself restore you and make you strong, firm and steadfast.'

1 Peter 5:8–10

Have you ever felt like your faith was under attack? Things go wrong, people point the finger, or you just can't shake a certain doubt you have. Well, you are not alone. There probably isn't a single Christian out there who hasn't felt like this at some point in their life. Paul got this and he encouraged Christians to 'take up the shield of faith, with which you can extinguish all the flaming arrows of the evil one' (Eph. 6:16).

In today's verses we have two top tips for how to use our shields of faith: be alert and resist. Let's not get so comfortable in life that we forget about the devil's tricks. And by being alert we will be ready to resist.

Now, resisting takes a lot of effort and strength. As we

mature as Christians we will grow stronger. Yet, no matter how old we are or what stage we're at, **we can't do it all in our own strength.**

Did you know that the Roman army designed their shields so that they could be interlocked? They could then advance with their shields locked together to form a solid wall, knowing that the enemy would find it difficult to force their way through them. In a similar way, Jesus wants us to be united in faith and love with other Christians and make a stand together.

We also have this brilliant promise at the end of our verse today: 'Christ … will himself restore you and make you strong'! With Jesus, we are a trillion times stronger than the devil!

Have you noticed a friend who is under pressure or doubting their faith at the moment? How could you support them? Could you give them a call or meet up with them? Prayer is powerful too; why not pray for them now?

Lord, when my faith is shaken or takes a hit, please strengthen me and put others alongside me who can help. Amen.

Face my fears

'Jesus said to his disciples, "Let us go across to the other side of the lake." So they … got into the boat … and they took him with them … Suddenly a strong wind blew up, and the waves began to spill over into the boat … Jesus was in the back of the boat, sleeping with his head on a pillow. The disciples woke him up and said, "Teacher, don't you care that we are about to die?" Jesus stood up and commanded the wind, "Be quiet!" and he said to the waves, "Be still!" The wind died down, and there was a great calm. Then Jesus said to his disciples, "Why are you frightened? Do you still have no faith?"'

Mark 4:35–41 (GNB)

What really scares you in everyday life? Being introduced to new people? Talking to your friends about your faith? Or something else? For the disciples in our verses today, they had a very good reason to be afraid. Their fear was a ferocious storm; for them, it was a life or death situation.

But what were they worrying about? They had *the* Jesus with them! But, and this is the key bit, notice what they said to Jesus: 'don't you care …?' And that is what we call doubt. They doubted

Jesus cared about them; they may have even doubted He had the power to save them.

Have you ever felt like that in the face of your fears? It's a trick of the devil to make us believe we are alone and unprotected. He wants us to doubt and run away from things. When we have the opportunity to tell our friends about Jesus, he wants us to run a mile because he knows our words have the power to bring people to faith!

So let's trust that God is always there – because He is! Let's have faith in His power to save. 'At all times carry faith as a shield' (Eph. 6:16, GNB).

Engage

God's power is much greater than the things we fear! With this in mind, take up this challenge: do something today that scares you! Step out of your comfort zone. Talk to your friend about church, talk to that person everyone else ignores. God is with you!

Pray

Jesus, when I am rocked by my fears, please let me know that You are standing right beside me. Help me keep my faith strong, whatever comes my way. Amen.

Hold that thought!

'For though we live in the world, we do not wage war as the world does. The weapons we fight with are not the weapons of the world. On the contrary, they have divine power to demolish strongholds. We demolish arguments and every pretension that sets itself up against the knowledge of God, and we take captive every thought to make it obedient to Christ.' **2 Corinthians 10:3–5**

We move onto our next piece of armour today! 'Take the helmet of salvation' (Eph. 6:17). First things first, why a helmet? Well, what does a helmet do? It protects a vitally important part of the wearer – their head! And inside our heads are our minds; our thoughts.

Have you ever heard of the idea that the mind can be like a battlefield? Negative thoughts seem to pop into our heads, seemingly out of nowhere sometimes. We can think up arguments with people and they develop and spiral, making us really angry! That is until we realise we made it all up!

We can create problems, imagine tragedies and hold onto bad memories. And our thoughts affect us. They eventually filter through to our beliefs and then to our behaviour.

We read a great verse today: 'take captive every thought to make it obedient to Christ.' This means that when a negative thought pops into your head, **you should 'grab it' and replace it with the truth.**

And that's where 'salvation' comes in. The truth is, and we can say this to every negative thought we may ever have, Jesus has saved us. He has saved us from sin; He has saved us from death! We don't need to keep turning back to any sinful ways, thinking 'Oh I can't help it', because we can now! We don't need to be fearful of tragedy or dying because we have the promise of heaven.

So by putting on the helmet of salvation we take every negative and damaging thought and replace them with good, true and faithful thoughts! And these will eventually spill out into the way we live our lives.

 Try this today. Be really aware of the thoughts that pop into your head. If they're negative, nip them in the bud straightaway by choosing to believe in God's truth instead.

Father, thank You for the Bible and for all the truth it holds. Help me to really use it today. Amen.

Highly or humbly?

'if you have any encouragement from being united with Christ, if any comfort from his love, if any common sharing in the Spirit, if any tenderness and compassion, then make my joy complete by being like-minded, having the same love, being one in spirit and of one mind. Do nothing out of selfish ambition or vain conceit. Rather, in humility value others above yourselves, not looking to your own interests but each of you to the interests of the others. In your relationships with one another, have the same mindset as Christ Jesus: who … made himself nothing by taking the very nature of a servant' **Philippians 2:1–7**

Staying with the helmet of salvation today, let's look at another idea about our thought life. More specifically, we're going to think about what we *think about ourselves*. We can find that we have to balance ourselves between not thinking too highly of ourselves, yet not thinking too low of ourselves either! And sometimes we feel like a yo-yo going up and down; feeling great and then feeling rubbish.

God's salvation not only saved us so that we can go to heaven one day. When we accept His salvation by accepting Jesus, we become *united* with Jesus. And we can have the same mindset as Him! We can see ourselves as He sees Himself: completely loved and valued by our heavenly Father! And from this we can see people, not for how they look or behave, but as the Father sees them, too. We can have compassion for them and be caring, putting their needs above our own.

There's a saying that goes: **Don't think less of yourself, just think about yourself less.** When we focus too much on ourselves – for example, our appearance or our circumstances – we can spiral into self-pity or pride. So let's look beyond ourselves, with the mindset of Jesus, and see what change we can bring to our thought life and to the lives of others!

Write the following down somewhere you will see every day …
I can have the same mindset as Jesus: I can know who I am (completely loved and accepted by God) and who God called me to be (completely loving and accepting of others).

God, help me to remember this today, and please help me to develop the mindset of Jesus, more and more, every day. Amen.

Fight back

'For the word of God is alive and active. Sharper than any double-edged sword, it penetrates even to dividing soul and spirit, joints and marrow; it judges the thoughts and attitudes of the heart. Nothing in all creation is hidden from God's sight. Everything is uncovered and laid bare before the eyes of him to whom we must give account.' **Hebrews 4:12–13**

So, we've looked at the belt of truth, the breastplate of righteousness, the shoes of peace, the shield of faith and the helmet of salvation! We've seen how these defend us from whatever the devil throws at us. Well, it's time to start fighting back! Our next piece of armour is 'the sword of the Spirit, which is the word of God' (Eph. 6:17).

The Word of God is known as two things. The first, perhaps more well-known, meaning is the Bible. In Matthew 4:1–11, we read about Jesus in wilderness. He was starving and exhausted, and the devil took this opportunity to try to tempt the Son of God. But Jesus would not be tempted! He used the Bible to counteract all of Satan's tricks. These verses are a brilliant example of how we can fight back, too – give them a read and see what you think!

Today's reading backs up the fact that the Bible is our weapon, 'sharper than any double-edged sword'. When we are tempted with negative thoughts or a selfish attitude, the Bible helps us get to the bottom of it so we can deal with it at the source.

The second meaning of 'the Word' is actually Jesus Himself (see John 1:1–18). **This is great news for us!** It means that, yes God speaks to us through the Bible, but we can speak to, hear from, and be in direct relationship with God Himself! We don't need to fight the devil on our own. We don't need to fight temptation on our own. Jesus is with us!

Engage **What do you need Jesus' help with right now? Don't fight *anything* on your own!**

Pray

Dear Lord Jesus, thank You for showing us that temptation does not have to lead to sin. We can fight anything with Your strength on our side. Amen.

Secret weapon

'Is anyone among you in trouble? Let them pray. Is anyone happy? Let them sing songs of praise. Is anyone among you ill? Let them call the elders of the church to pray over them and anoint them with oil in the name of the Lord. And the prayer offered in faith will make the sick person well; the Lord will raise them up. If they have sinned, they will be forgiven. Therefore confess your sins to each other and pray for each other so that you may be healed. The prayer of a righteous person is powerful and effective.' **James 5:13–16**

It's one thing to have all you need to complete a task – the tools, the equipment, the kit – but it's another to complete the task well. When Paul wrote about the armour of God, he also gave us the key that would allow us to use it to its full potential: 'pray in the Spirit on all occasions with all kinds of prayers and requests' (Eph. 6:18).

Prayer is simply talking with and listening to God. It's a direct line to our all-powerful and completely loving Creator. When we pray for miracles, when we pray for someone to get better, when we pray for God to open a door, God answers and the results can be completely amazing!

Today's verses give us an idea of how, when and why we should pray. When we're in trouble or ill, or in need of forgiveness, we can talk to God. But not just then! Also, simply when we're happy! **We can talk to God all the time.**

Why should we pray? Because it develops our relationship with God. We get to know Him more, and so we can understand ourselves and life more. Also, we should pray because, as 'righteous' people (made right with God by believing in Jesus), our prayers really do make a difference – they are 'powerful and effective'!

Engage

Paul goes on to say: 'With this in mind, be alert and always keep on praying for all the Lord's people' (Eph. 6:18). Who do you know who could really do with God's help right now? If you can't think of anyone, look out for someone today and pray for them. Really believe that your prayers are 'powerful and effective' because they are.

Pray

Lord, thank You so much that I can talk to You anytime, anywhere and for any reason. Amen.

What should I wear?

'put on the full armour of God … Stand firm then, with the belt of truth buckled round your waist, with the breastplate of righteousness in place, and with your feet fitted with the readiness that comes from the gospel of peace. In addition to all this, take up the shield of faith, with which you can extinguish all the flaming arrows of the evil one. Take the helmet of salvation and the sword of the Spirit, which is the word of God.'

Ephesians 6:13–17

As we've come to the end of our chapter on the armour of God, let's recap what we've found out and hear one final nugget of advice!

Here's each piece of armour, along with how we can use them …

With *the belt of truth* we resist the devil's lies and replace them with God's truth.

With *the breastplate of righteousness* we protect the belief in our hearts that we are made right with God through Jesus.

With *the shoes of peace* we are kept in God's perfect peace no matter how 'un-peaceful' our surroundings are.

With *the shield of faith* we protect ourselves from doubt, so that we can completely trust in God's promises.

With *the helmet of salvation* we protect our minds from negative or selfish thinking, knowing we are saved by Jesus, and can have the same mindset as Him.

With *the sword of the Spirit (the Word)* we can fight back against the devil, knowing we have Jesus on our side.

So what's that last bit of advice? Well, notice how today's reading starts: 'put on'. It might seem obvious, but the armour of God does not automatically become a part of us when we become Christians; it comes *available* to us. **It's our choice whether we use it all or not** and so, if we do want to (who wouldn't?!) we have to make a conscious effort to 'put it on'.

Engage

Why not write out this recap list of the armour of God onto a piece of paper and stick it inside your wardrobe? Every time you go to pick out your clothes for the day, you'll be reminded to 'put on the full armour of God' too!

Pray

Father God, thank You so much for making these amazing defences and weapons available to me. I am in a fight every day, but with Your help, I can overcome anything. Amen.

'Now when Jesus saw the crowds, he went up on a mountainside and sat down. His disciples came to him, and he began to teach them.' **Matthew 5:1–2**

Deliberately Different

The more we get to know Jesus and the way He lived, the more we realise that not a lot of people today are following His way. This can be a real challenge for us as Christians. The temptation to follow the crowd, go with the flow and give in to peer pressure is enormous! So where do we start? Paul wrote something really interesting about this: 'Do not conform to the pattern of this world, but be transformed by the renewing of your mind' (Rom. 12:2).

Over this chapter we are going to 'renew our minds' by getting stuck into a really helpful part of the Bible. In Matthew 5, 6 and 7, Jesus gives what is known as 'the Sermon on the Mount'. In it, Jesus outlines how we can live God's way; how we can be deliberately different to the way of the world.

So what's the real difference between God's way and the world's way?

In short, the world's way is to look after No. 1 (yourself) and do want you think makes you happy – after all, 'you only live once'! But God's way is to follow the real No. 1 (God!) because He knows what will truly fulfil you, and live as an example of Jesus so that others might come to know Him themselves. After all, we only live *this* life once, but we have an eternity in heaven to look forward to.

So let's go God's way, not simply to draw attention to ourselves for the sake of it, but to be an example, a spokesperson, for God!

 What do you think about this subject of being deliberately different? Are you convinced we should be? Why not talk to an older Christian about it and discuss what you both believe?

Father God, please speak to me as I go on to read about Jesus' guidance for life. Please renew my mind so that I can see more clearly that I don't have to go with flow; I can choose the way I live my life. Amen.

Be happy!

'[Jesus] said; "Blessed are the poor in spirit, for theirs is the kingdom of heaven. Blessed are those who mourn, for they will be comforted. Blessed are the meek, for they will inherit the earth. Blessed are those who hunger and thirst for righteousness, for they will be filled. Blessed are the merciful, for they will be shown mercy. Blessed are the pure in heart, for they will see God. Blessed are the peacemakers, for they will be called children of God."' **Matthew 5:3–9**

Jesus was genuinely different. And He taught His disciples to be deliberately different too. Our verses today are the first words Jesus said in this teaching session (the Sermon on the Mount). You might think it's a bit odd at first. So let's unpack it a little.

To be blessed, in a way, is to be happy. It's a very special type of happiness because it does not rely on good things happening to us. No matter what life throws at us we can experience this joy of knowing Jesus and putting Him first.

So today's verses, in other words, would go a little like this:

We experience this amazing happiness when we are …

- *Content with God alone* – not looking to the things we own on earth to make us happy.
- *Humble* – listening to God and to others.
- *Eager to learn what's right* – and live it.
- *Kind and don't hold grudges.*
- *Pure* – in our thinking, what we read and watch, and in our relationships.
- *Peacemakers* – not troublemakers.

It's important to know that this isn't like a pick 'n' mix, where we can choose some and not others – **this is a person to be!** Jesus lived what He preached. He was the walking, talking version of these qualities and made a deep impact on all He met.

Which characteristics do you think you need more of? Humility? Kindness? Contentment? Through growing and learning in God, you can develop these! And you know what? Not only will you be blessed, people will notice these qualities in you and may very well want to know what makes you so different!

Lord Jesus, please help me to develop these brilliant qualities. I want to be the person You made me to be so that I can be a shining example of You. Amen.

Be faithful

'Blessed are those who are persecuted because of righteousness, for theirs is the kingdom of heaven. Blessed are you when people insult you, persecute you … because of me. Rejoice and be glad, because great is your reward in heaven'
Matthew 5:10–12

When Jesus was 'Mr Popular' with the crowds, the disciples wanted to be seen with Him. They even fought to get the 'top spot' next to Him (they obviously didn't understand that God doesn't have favourites!). But when they got to Jerusalem and the locals moved in to hurt Jesus, they deserted Him. Peter denied, three times, that he was a friend of Jesus. Ouch!

So are we different? At a big Christian event, are we there at the front, worshipping God with all our hearts, but back in the classroom, are we keeping our faith completely to ourselves?

Fear of rejection is very real. Worries about what others might think, say or do, prompt us to compromise. What does Jesus say about this?

When being real for God means you're on the receiving end of insults, hurts and lies – be happy! Be honoured that you are getting the same reaction as those who have lived for God in the past. Those who side with Jesus get treated like Jesus.

Jesus saw rejection as an issue to be handled with joy. He didn't readjust His lifestyle and tone down His beliefs to avoid crucifixion – **His priority was to be faithful and obedient to God.**

And it's really a question of who we are trying to impress – our peers or God? If staying in with the crowd is more important, we'll become more like the crowd. But by following Jesus bravely and wholeheartedly, we'll be different – deliberately different!

Talk with other Christians about the pressures you all face. Encourage each other and be there to help those facing peer pressure or even bullying.

God, I value Your friendship above everything else, please help me to live a life that proves this. When I am under pressure to deny You, please help me to stand strong and be faithful to You. When I am mocked or rejected by others, please comfort and bless me. Amen.

Be ... salty?!

'You are the salt of the earth. But if the salt loses its saltiness, how can it be made salty again? It is no longer good for anything, except to be thrown out and trampled underfoot.' **Matthew 5:13**

What an extraordinary verse! Before we skim over it and move onto the next, as we might be tempted to do, let's dig a little deeper into this seemingly bonkers bit of Scripture!

In Bible times, when Jesus said these words, salt was a very versatile and useful ingredient. For starters, people didn't use fridges or freezers (as they had nowhere to plug them in!) and in the hot climate, meat started to give off a horrible whiff and soon went rotten. The only way to keep meat fresh was to pack it in salt.

Salt was also rubbed into wounds to stop them becoming infected (where we get the expression 'rubbing salt into a wound' from). It stung but it kept the wound clean.

By using the analogy of salt, Jesus was teaching His disciples – and us – that we as Christians have a number of brilliant uses that we can bring to help the world around us – if only we're aware of them!

Just as salt keeps meat from going off or prevents wounds from becoming infected, we need to keep each other in check, standing up against infectious habits and cleaning up our attitudes.

Jesus went on to warn that salt could lose its flavour. Damp salt was useless and thrown on the floor. It was stored in one of the temple storerooms and sprinkled on the slippery marble courtyards during wet weather. Everyone trampled over useless salt.

So the message is, **know what you're capable of** as a follower of Jesus and daughter of God! Don't ever forget it (lose your saltiness)! You can be radically helpful to those in need.

It's a brilliant idea to have someone at church – your youth leader perhaps – who you can ask to help keep you 'in check'. They can pray for you and ask you how you're doing in particular areas of your life. Could you find someone like this, or, if you already have someone, could you speak to them more often? God knows how much we need each other; that's why He's placed these people around us!

Lord, if someone needs my help today, please point them out to me. I want to put my 'saltiness' to good use right now. Amen.

Be a light

'You are the light of the world. A town built on a hill cannot be hidden. Neither do people light a lamp and put it under a bowl. Instead they put it on its stand, and it gives light to everyone in the house. In the same way, let your light shine before others, that they may see your good deeds and glorify your Father in heaven.'
Matthew 5:14–16

What is light good for? Well, when light shines, whether it's a great big floodlight or a tiny flicker of a flame, it has a certain effect. It reveals what the darkness was hiding. Again, Jesus is using a visual idea to teach us something about ourselves as Christians.

There is a lot of 'darkness' in our world – in other words, a lot of evil, nasty and unjust things. And when people live in this darkness, the saddest part is that they don't even realise it. They go about their lives believing 'this is just how things are'. But when God comes along, He shines His light into their world so that they can see the life they're living for what it really is, and find their way to God. And God wants to use us as carriers of His light!

Depending on our personalities, the idea of 'shining' might fill us with fear rather than excitement. But we don't need to panic. God chose our personalities; He knows what we find hard and He will provide us with whatever we need to do the things He's called us to do. **It may nudge us out of our comfort zones** from time to time but when opportunity comes, we have a choice to hide our light or let it out. And as today's verses say, you don't put a light under a bowl!

 Engage

What do you think about the idea of 'shining' for God? Do you think it means being the star in a school play more than it does helping someone in need? We can shine through anything, every day!

Pray

Dear Lord Jesus, thank You for reminding me that there is darkness around me, but through me, You can shine and help people find the way to You. Amen.

Be loved

'Do not think that I have come to abolish the Law or the Prophets; I have not come to abolish them but to fulfil them. For truly I tell you, until heaven and earth disappear, not the smallest letter, not the least stroke of a pen, will by any means disappear from the Law until everything is accomplished. Therefore … whoever practises and teaches these commands will be called great in the kingdom of heaven. For I tell you that unless your righteousness surpasses that of the Pharisees and the teachers of the law, you will certainly not enter the kingdom of heaven.' **Matthew 5:17–20**

If one thing was going to put you off following God it was the Pharisees. They were ruled by rules. It wasn't the Ten Commandments that were the problem but the 600 dos and don'ts they added to the list! And they made themselves feel good by looking down their noses at those who broke them.

They thought that you had to earn your place in heaven. But they had it all wrong. The truth is, God loves us so much that He sent Jesus to pay for our place; we just have to accept Him into our hearts.

Now some people might stop there and think, 'OK, so I can live however I want then and it doesn't matter.' In today's verses we see that this is incorrect! There is still a way God wants us to live and obeying Him is actually for *our* benefit. Jesus didn't break any of God's rules – not once – but if He needed to break any taboo or daft tradition to reach out to those in need, He did (like healing someone on the Sabbath). Jesus played things God's way, following His rules, not to feel superior to others, but **because He knew of the Father's love for Him** and He wanted to love Him back.

Sometimes it's easy to fall into the trap of living out a second-hand list of dos and don'ts (especially if you've been brought up in a Christian family). Do you need to get your relationship with God round the right way: accepting God's love first and then following His rules in response?

Jesus, please help me to get this round the right way, just as You did. Help my relationship with You to grow stronger so that I understand, more and more, why You lived the way You did. Amen.

Be reconciled

'I tell you that anyone who is angry with a brother or sister will be subject to judgment … Therefore, if you are offering your gift at the altar and there remember that your brother or sister has something against you, leave your gift there in front of the altar. First go and be reconciled to them; then come and offer your gift. Settle matters quickly with your adversary who is taking you to court. Do it while you are still together on the way'

Matthew 5:22–25

Reconciled. What a word! In case you didn't know, it means to restore a friendship by saying sorry and settling an argument. Arguments with friends can be the worst! Jesus' advice? **Settle it quickly!** It's true, the longer you leave it, the deeper the hurt goes and the harder it will be to sort it out.

If you are a Christian, it doesn't necessarily make these situations any easier, or mean you're less likely to fall out with someone. We're all human after all. But what we do have as Christians is our amazing relationship with God.

God made us to be in relationship with others. He knows how great friendship can be – and how much we need it to thrive in life. Perhaps that's why Jesus stresses the importance of making up with our friends after a fight. And He does so by giving us a priority list:

1. Go make amends with the person
2. Worship God

Wow! That shows us just how important reconciliation is!

So, when we've decided to go and make amends, how do we do it? Well, we can sort out any bitterness and hurt with those concerned by showing forgiveness. If it was your fault, say sorry, if it wasn't your fault, say you're sorry for the way the argument went. (We all say things we don't mean when things get a little heated.)

'Impossible!' you may think? But not with God's help. The world says, 'Get even.' Jesus says, 'Forgive.' That's so deliberately different!

 Have you had an argument with someone recently? Have you made amends yet? Or do you know someone who has been in a nasty fight? What advice could you give them?

Lord, please help me not to be stubborn or unforgiving when I fall out with others, but prompt me to sort the matter out straightaway. Amen.

Be a bit 'over the top'

'If your right eye causes you to stumble, gouge it out and throw it away. It is better for you to lose one part of your body than for your whole body to be thrown into hell. And if your right hand causes you to stumble, cut it off and throw it away. It is better for you to lose one part of your body than for your whole body to go into hell.' **Matthew 5:29–30**

First we should say that these verses aren't meant to be taken too literally! So before you poke yourself in the eye, let's get to the bottom of what Jesus was really saying.

'Causes you to stumble' in other words means 'causes you to sin'. Jesus is talking about temptation.

Have you ever heard someone say, 'Don't give the devil a foothold'? Sometimes we find that we're particularly vulnerable to a certain temptation. For some it's food, for others it's fancying too many people, and so on. Whatever it is, know that the devil is very aware of your 'weakness' and the more you 'play with fire', the more 'footholds' you're giving to him. He 'climbs up', becoming a stronger influence in your life. But don't fear, with the Holy Spirit living in us, we have the power to knock him off in seconds!

But how do we prevent the devil having such a hold on us in the first place? Let's go back to Jesus' words in today's verses – which are actually surprisingly practical! If 'your eye' causes you to give in to temptation and so sin, 'cut it out'. Try this: replace 'your eye' in that sentence with whatever tempts you most. Then think about a practical action you can take and put it in the place of 'cut it out'. Here's an example: if what you watch on TV causes you to sin, stop watching certain programmes, reduce how many hours you watch a day, or remove your TV from your bedroom!

You might think this is a bit 'over the top' but sometimes we have to be when it comes to temptation. And, it is true, you do need a lot of inner strength to do this. **But with the Holy Spirit it is possible.**

Engage **What tempts you the most?**
Today, what practical steps could
you take to overcome it?

Pray

Holy Spirit, please empower me today to make a stand against temptation. Amen.

Be a promise-keeper

'I tell you, do not swear an oath at all: either by heaven, for it is God's throne; or by the earth, for it is his footstool; or by Jerusalem, for it is the city of the Great King. And do not swear by your head, for you cannot make even one hair white or black. All you need to say is simply "Yes," or "No"; anything beyond this comes from the evil one.' **Matthew 5:34–37**

Have you ever promised something and got one of those 'I'll believe it when I see it' looks? Often it's because people have trusted us in the past and we've let them down. And when we sense that people doubt us, we sometimes say things like, 'No, I mean it' or 'I swear I'll do it', or come up with daft phrases like 'cross my heart'.

In Jesus' day people would make promises and swear to keep them in 'heaven's name' or 'by Jerusalem'.

Jesus wanted His followers to be different – to be honest – and not make promises they wouldn't or couldn't keep. A 'yes' should mean 'I'll do it' and a 'no' should mean 'I won't' – **simple as that!**

Some people think it's smart to con people or smooth talk to get their way. They spin the yarn to pull the wool over our eyes. But we soon learn not to trust them. Jesus wants us to be deliberately different – saying what we mean and meaning what we say. Delivering on our promises. It's a powerful witness to be someone who keeps their word.

Engage

Have you made any promises lately?
Tick the one/s you have:

- [ ] To do my homework
- [ ] To be kind to my family
- [ ] To tidy my bedroom
- [ ] To pay back some money
- [ ] To be home at a certain time
- [ ] Other _____

Try to keep them today/this week!

Pray

God, please help me to always keep my word so that people will know that I'm trustworthy. Amen.

Be grace-full

'If anyone slaps you on the right cheek, turn to them the other cheek also. And if anyone wants to sue you and take your shirt, hand over your coat as well. If anyone forces you to go one mile, go with them two miles. Give to the one who asks you, and do not turn away from the one who wants to borrow from you.'

Matthew 5:39–42

In Old Testament days if someone punched out your front teeth you had the right to knock out theirs. Whatever injury had been inflicted on you, you could inflict on them. Jesus had a very different approach – don't seek revenge, look to forgive instead.

The 'turn the other cheek' attitude doesn't mean that when you get hurt you come back for more. It's a brave reaction that refuses to strike back with anything but love – it's called grace.

Jesus was treated very badly, but He prayed from the cross, 'Father, forgive them …' That was radical grace!

What about that extra mile bit (so that's where the saying, 'Go the extra mile' comes from!)? Well, in Jesus' time, an occupying Roman soldier could force any Jew to carry his kit for a mile. The Jews hated it. At any moment they could be picked and made to hike some squaddie's heavy gear wherever he wanted it. You can imagine their reactions – moaning, complaining, being resentful. Well, again Jesus had a mind-blowing alternative reaction – 'go an extra mile'. And it wasn't to do with the distance but their reaction to hassle and hard work. Instead of complaining, they should **be helpful and give their best – even to their enemies.**

Jesus willingly gave everything, including His life, for us. Imagine what an impact it would make if instead of groaning at hassles and hard work, we deliberately went out of our way to help and get things done.

 Our reaction to hurt or hassle gets noticed!
Has anyone hurt you recently, or in the past? Talk to a leader at church about it and ask them to help you pray and forgive that person.
Has anyone asked you to complete a job or task? How can you go the extra mile and do it all with a grace-full attitude?

Dear God, please help me develop an attitude like Jesus, full of grace and forgiveness. It's such a powerful witness for You. Amen.

Be top-secret (Part 1)

'Be careful not to practise your righteousness in front of others to be seen by them. If you do, you will have no reward from your Father in heaven. So when you give to the needy, do not announce it with trumpets, as the hypocrites do in the synagogues and on the streets, to be honoured by others. Truly I tell you, they have received their reward in full. But when you give to the needy, do not let your left hand know what your right hand is doing, so that your giving may be in secret. Then your Father, who sees what is done in secret, will reward you.' **Matthew 6:1–4**

The Pharisees, who were comfortably well-off, made a big show of putting money in the Temple treasury. They would announce what they were doing over the PA system (a trumpet), pull out a bag of shekels and jingle them around, wait for an applause and then give their gift … (Pretty much!)

They gave selfishly. Their motive wasn't to help the poor but to help themselves and their image.

Jesus had a radically different way of helping those in need: just do it – and don't make a song and dance about it.

It begs the question: **how much do we do for others when there's no one watching?** That not only applies to our money but to our talents too.

Jesus went out of His way to meet and help the poor, sick and rejected. He channelled the majority of His time and resources into those who couldn't repay Him. He healed but never put on a show for publicity. He gave without letting others know how much.

Engage

Be honest with yourself, do you sometimes help people or give to the offering at church so that others will see and think highly of you? It's so tempting to do so. Why don't you do something kind and helpful this week – and do it as secretly as you can?

Pray

Lord, Your opinion of me is far greater than anyone else's. When I give my time, effort, talents and money – it's all for You. Amen.

Be top-secret (Part 2)

'when you pray, go into your room, close the door and pray to your Father … who sees what is done in secret … do not keep on babbling like pagans, for they think they will be heard because of their many words. Do not be like them, for your Father knows what you need before you ask him. This, then, is how you should pray: "Our Father in heaven, hallowed be your name, your kingdom come, your will be done, on earth as it is in heaven. Give us today our daily bread. And forgive us our debts, as we also have forgiven our debtors. And lead us not into temptation, but deliver us from the evil one."' **Matthew 6:6–13**

The religious posers liked to pray seven times a day – in public, where everyone could see them. And many of their 'performances' were worthy of Oscar nominations! They thought that God was impressed with long dramatic prayers.

Jesus was different. **Prayer wasn't about posing, but power.** And He would often retreat to a quiet place to spend quality time alone with God. It was during such top-secret prayer times that Jesus made key decisions as to what He should do next. Prayer made such a difference to Jesus' life that the disciples wanted to get empowered – the Jesus way.

The Lord's Prayer is so familiar to many of us that we tend to forget what it can really mean. Here's what the prayer tells us, in other words …

Come as a daughter, wanting to learn from your heavenly Father. Show Him respect and lift Him up, He is the Lord of all. Tell Him that you want to fit into His plans instead of squeezing Him into yours. Ask for help where you need it now. Be real with Him about your disobedience. Be open with Him about the actions you have taken to forgive others. And ask Him to help you to never give up on doing good or resisting temptation.

Engage   **How often do you go to talk to God in secret? Do you have a special place that you always go to? If not, could you find one and plan to visit it as often as you can?**

Pray

Heavenly Father, thank You for the amazing ability I have to talk to You whenever, wherever I want. I will not take it for granted. Amen.

Be a treasure-hunter

'Do not store up for yourselves treasures on earth, where moths and vermin destroy, and where thieves break in and steal. But store up for yourselves treasures in heaven … For where your treasure is, there your heart will be also ... No one can serve two masters. Either you will hate the one and love the other … You cannot serve both God and Money … Therefore I tell you, do not worry about your life, what you will eat or drink; or about your body, what you will wear … But seek first his kingdom and his righteousness, and all these things will be given to you as well.' **Matthew 6:19–21,24–25,33**

The bigwigs in Israel had land, servants, big houses, loads of livestock and the top seat in the synagogue. And some of the disciples hoped for the get-rich-quick lifestyle if Jesus became king. But Jesus had other ideas – and a radical view of status, image and possessions.

Treasures on earth are so short-lived and temporary. Looks fade, metal rusts and today's fashions quickly become 'so yesterday'. Jesus didn't get hung up on these things. He lived simply and with the freedom to meet people and help them. The reason? He knew that it was a much better investment to put His time and effort into the things of heaven. If you're wondering what 'treasures in heaven' mean, you could look at it this way: **what do we take with us to heaven?** Our clothes, our houses, our trophies? No! It's our souls that go to heaven and while we're on earth we can be the ones who lead other people to heaven too. How do we do this? By following Jesus' example. He went where God wanted Him – doing what God asked of Him.

When we do the same, we make an impact on those around us. And we never miss out. The world rewards those who help themselves but God rewards those who help others.

 What things are at the top of your priority list right now? Have a think about them. Are they things of earth or things of heaven? If you're not sure, why not talk to some of your Christian friends about it?

Dear Lord, thank You for this reminder that, in the grand scheme of things, what I wear and possess is not really that important compared to leading others to You. Help me with my priorities today. Amen.

Be an optician

'Do not judge, or you too will be judged. For in the same way as you judge others, you will be judged, and with the measure you use, it will be measured to you. Why do you look at the speck of sawdust in your brother's eye and pay no attention to the plank in your own eye? How can you say to your brother, "Let me take the speck out of your eye," when all the time there is a plank in your own eye? You hypocrite, first take the plank out of your own eye, and then you will see clearly to remove the speck from your brother's eye.' **Matthew 7:1–5**

'**Have** you heard what *she* did?' … 'What is she *wearing*?' … 'I *knew* she was going to mess up.'

Judging others. It's a trap we can all fall into. But when we think about it, **what good are we doing by pointing out other people's flaws,** especially when it's behind their backs?!

Pointing the finger can make us feel better about ourselves, but only for a little while, and really it's another thing that can get in the way between us and God.

Jesus saw this in people and so He taught a deliberately different way of living. What a great picture the sawdust and the plank is! It really highlights the foolishness of judging others.

So what should we do instead? Well, be an example. 'Take out the plank' by being honest with yourself, with God and perhaps with another Christian you trust. When we own up to our mistakes, we're opening up the opportunity for others to be humble and honest too. And we'll be a far more appealing witness of Jesus.

A lot of people are put off Christianity because of this idea that Christians are hypocritical – or sadly, have actually experienced being judged by Christians themselves. Well, let's be different, the way God intended, and show people how Jesus really wanted us to live.

What would you say to someone who didn't want to come to church because they believed they would be judged? Why not talk about this issue with some of your friends?

Lord Jesus, please help me to fight the temptation to judge others. I have my own flaws to deal with, and with Your help I can put them right. Thank You. Amen.

Simply be a daughter

'Ask and it will be given to you; seek and you will find; knock and the door will be opened to you. For everyone who asks receives; the one who seeks finds; and to the one who knocks, the door will be opened. Which of you, if your son asks for bread, will give him a stone? Or if he asks for a fish, will give him a snake? If you ... know how to give good gifts to your children, how much more will your Father in heaven give good gifts to those who ask him!' **Matthew 7:7–11**

Take a deep breath and relax! This chapter on being deliberately different is a challenging one! Well, today, let these verses reassure you and give you the strength you need to live out these dynamically different ways of living our lives. Because today we remember that we are daughters of the King of kings and Lord of lords!

Earthly fathers are not perfect, yet many of them know how to love their daughters through giving gifts and saying loving words. But our Father in heaven *is* perfect – completely perfect! His love for us is SO huge, it's quite frankly mind-blowing! He knows exactly what we need in life – and He knows what makes us happy.

All these things you've been learning about are pretty impossible to achieve without first **knowing how much you are loved.** Perhaps bad experiences in the past have led you to believe that God doesn't care. We can sometimes think a bad situation is God punishing us as well. This is simply not true; today's verses promise us otherwise.

If we need something today, all we have to do is ask! If we're looking for an answer or simply to experience the presence of God (which is amazing) all we need to do is look!

Engage

What do you want to ask for or experience from God today? Do you need a new burst of energy to keep walking His way? Do you want to see one of your friends come to know Jesus? You are God's daughter, be bold in your prayers!

Pray

Heavenly Father, I believe that You give good gifts to Your children. You never want to hurt me and You care so much about me. Thank You. Amen.

Be a signpost

'Enter through the narrow gate. For wide is the gate and broad is the road that leads to destruction, and many enter through it. But small is the gate and narrow the road that leads to life, and only a few find it.' **Matthew 7:13–14**

Jesus painted this picture of a narrow road that led to a narrow gate, and a wide road that led to a wide gate. He was illustrating the way to heaven and the way to hell in a really clear and eye-opening way.

Have you ever thought of it like this before? It makes so much sense when we think about how much pressure there is to follow the crowd.

The broad way is popular and easy to walk. You don't stand out; you fit in with the crowd. You feel comfortable because, after all, everyone else is heading in the same direction. Could all these people really have it all wrong? According to Jesus – 'Yes'.

Turning from the popular route to follow Jesus can be a bumpy ride and sometimes a lonely one too – full of ups and downs. But the narrow way isn't for the narrow-minded but the brave. It's for those prepared to trust Jesus, not the crowd. Those prepared to let God take them in a new direction – **on a road that leads to heaven.**

If you've accepted Jesus into your heart and have decided to follow Him, you can be sure that you are walking on the right road. It certainly won't always be easy, but knowing your destination should spur you on! And now you have a vitally important job to do too: to show others that there is another way. God is looking out for those of us who are willing to reach out, to be there for others and to lovingly bring them to know Jesus for themselves.

As well as helping those on the wide road move over to the narrow one, we can look out for our Christian friends too. Who could you encourage today? Who needs picking up or reminding of the amazing future we have to look forward to?

God, please help me to be a risk-taker – deliberately diverting people towards the path that leads to You. Amen.

Be an architect

'"everyone who hears these words of mine and puts them into practice is like a wise man who built his house on the rock. The rain came down …the winds blew and beat against that house; yet it did not fall, because it had its foundation on the rock. But everyone who … does not put them into practice is like a foolish man who built his house on sand. The rain came down … the winds blew and beat against that house, and it fell with a great crash." When Jesus had finished saying these things, the crowds were amazed at his teaching, because he taught as one who had authority' **Matthew 7:24–29**

We've come to the end of our chapter on being deliberately different. And today, we read the very last part of Jesus' Sermon on the Mount. Jesus often used storytelling to illustrate His teaching. It was not only a great way of helping people understand His point, but it was far more easy to remember too!

So Jesus told this story of two builders. The first one clearly knew the importance of strong foundations and so he put that theory into practice. Despite the higher cost and greater effort digging into rock would cause, he knew it would be worth it in the end, so he dug deep.

He was building for the future – he knew his work would last.

The second builder also knew how important it was to have a strong foundation – who doesn't? But he couldn't be bothered to dig deep into the rock! Too much like hard work. So he built on sand instead, thinking 'life's too short to sort things out deep down'.

Having told the story, Jesus goes on to make a telling point. Those who hear God's teaching but ignore Him are like the builder who built on sand. Those who listen to Him and put His deliberately different lifestyle into action are those building a strong foundation – one that will last.

Engage **So where does that leave you? Are you prepared to dig deep into your Bible, put it into practice and help others? Do you want to make an impact that lasts?**

Pray

Jesus, thank You for Your teaching that is so different to the way of the world. Help me not to ignore it or choose the easy way out. I want my whole life to be built on You and Your example. Amen.

Powered by Praise

'Shout for joy to the LORD, all the earth. Worship the LORD with gladness; come before him with joyful songs. Know that the LORD is God. It is he who made us, and we are his; we are his people, the sheep of his pasture. Enter his gates with thanksgiving and his courts with praise; give thanks to him and praise his name. For the LORD is good and his love endures for ever; his faithfulness continues through all generations.'

Psalm 100:1–5

Praise and worship is an important, exciting and really valuable part of being a Christian, just as much as prayer and reading the Bible is! There is power in worshipping God. When we lift Him up, He pours out His blessings. And it's also a way of putting the devil in his place (he hates it when we worship God!). Over this chapter we are going to explore what worship is and how it can strengthen our relationship with God and empower us in our general everyday life.

Today, we start off by thinking of worship as a journey – go with it!

In Bible times, a trip to the temple was a journey of worship for pilgrims. When they climbed to the gates of Jerusalem they recited psalms. As they went through the gates, they shouted prayers of thanksgiving before heading to one of several courts where they praised God. Verse 3 in the reading gives us a brilliant reason to praise God ... He made us! AND we are His!

It can be really helpful to think of a time of worship as a journey to meet with God. Our journey of worship can start with thanksgiving – as we reflect on all that God has done for us and thank Him. Then we should take our eyes off ourselves and fully focus on God and who He is.

Engage

Why not worship God right now? Write down a list of all the things you're thankful for. Go through the list, thanking God for each one! Then write a list of some of the amazing qualities of God you can think of (eg, faithful, kind, loving) and praise Him for who He is!

Pray

Lord God, You are worthy of all my worship. Please help me learn more about praise and worship, over the next few days. Amen.

Something to shout about

'Come, let us sing for joy to the LORD; let us shout aloud to the Rock of our salvation. Let us come before him with thanksgiving and extol him with music and song. For the LORD is the great God, the great King above all gods. In his hand are the depths of the earth, and the mountain peaks belong to him. The sea is his, for he made it, and his hands formed the dry land. Come, let us bow down in worship, let us kneel before the Lord our Maker; for he is our God and we are the people of his pasture, the flock under his care.' **Psalm 95:1–7**

Some of us would take any excuse to shout about something, while others would prefer to stay quiet! But sometimes, when it comes to lifting up God, **we need to turn up the volume!** Today's verses encourage us to 'shout aloud' to God.

First, let's think about the more obvious time of worship – during church services. When the music's playing and the words are up on the screen, do you throw yourself into worship or do you tend to hold back? When you really grasp that God is completely amazing and that He *really* loves you, you'll find that you don't really care what other people might think of you when you lift up your hands, sing your heart out or dance like crazy! And that's great!

Another time we can get loud is when we're talking to God. Jesus spent many quiet hours praying to God but there were times when He expressed His deep feeling with a loud voice. On the cross, despite the difficulty of getting breath, He called out to God to forgive those who were killing Him. So we can lift our voices to God as a way of expressing ourselves to Him – when we're ecstatically happy, desperately sad or anywhere in between. He can take our excitement, anger or whatever emotion we're feeling!

Don't hold back!

 Are you naturally loud or shy? If you're the loud type why not think about using that to lift God up? If you're quite shy, could you push yourself out of your comfort zone and get into the worship at your church more? God deserves our all!

Lord God, please give me the courage to not hold back from worshipping You. Amen.

The best way to boast

'I will extol the LORD at all times; his praise will always be on my lips. I will glory in the LORD; let the afflicted hear and rejoice. Glorify the LORD with me: let us exalt his name together. I sought the LORD, and he answered me; he delivered me from all my fears. Those who look to him are radiant; their faces are never covered with shame. This poor man called, and the LORD heard him; he saved him out of all his troubles. The angel of the LORD encamps around those who fear him, and he delivers them. Taste and see that the LORD is good; blessed is the one who takes refuge in him.' **Psalm 34:1–8**

It is tempting to take the credit for the things God has given us and sing our own praises, 'I can do this … I can do that …'

King David, who wrote many of the psalms, made a habit of boasting about God. 'God has done this … God has done that.' He was always telling others what God had done and was doing in his life. Instead of singing his own praises, he gave God centre stage.

Today's verses tell us something brilliant that happens when we boast about God – others are helped. When David praised God, people stopped worrying about their problems and tuned in to God. As they praised God's name, their fears disappeared. Faces that were etched with sadness, radiated happiness. Other kings encouraged their subjects to bow and honour them, but King David wanted his to see 'that the LORD is good'.

Paul the apostle said this: 'If I must boast, I will boast of the things that show my weakness' (2 Cor. 11:30). **He wanted others to see that God was his strength.**

Engage It's great to share with others what God is doing in your life. Today, find a friend or family member who loves Jesus and encourage them by boasting about God's goodness!

Pray

Heavenly Father, You deserve all my praise. When I am tempted to boast, help me to boast about You instead! Amen.

When's a good time?

'Be very careful, then, how you live – not as unwise but as wise, making the most of every opportunity, because the days are evil. Therefore do not be foolish, but understand what the Lord's will is. Do not get drunk on wine, which leads to debauchery. Instead, be filled with the Spirit, speaking to one another with psalms, hymns, and songs from the Spirit. Sing and make music from your heart to the Lord, always giving thanks to God the Father for everything, in the name of our Lord Jesus Christ.' **Ephesians 5:15–20**

It's one thing to praise God when you have got it all together but it's another thing to praise Him when things go wrong.

Obviously, things in life may not always go the way we want them to. In fact, sometimes bad things do happen and it would be crazy to pretend everything's all lovely-jubbly in these situations.

God doesn't expect us to be thankful for the struggles in our lives – but to be thankful *in* those struggles. You don't thank God that you got soaking wet walking to school, that the person you fancy is going out with your best friend, that your mum won't let you play your music at full volume or that your exam results are poor. But you can be thankful that God knows you, holds you and is with you.

In our reading today, Paul gives some practical advice to help us to be thankful in *all* situations:

1. Find out what God wants you to do and do it (v17).
2. Don't turn away from God to drown your sorrows (v18).
3. Be filled with the Holy Spirit (v18).
4. Sing to God from your heart (v19).
5. Meet with other Christians to worship God together (v19).

Why don't you try these ideas out this week?

 A good time to praise God is right now! No matter your current situation, why don't you praise God today? Simply saying 'You are good, Lord!' is praise in itself.

Lord, You really are good, all the time, but when my life is not going so good, please help me to stay close to You through it all. Amen.

What's your outlook?

'Rejoice in the Lord always. I will say it again: rejoice! Let your gentleness be evident to all. The Lord is near. Do not be anxious about anything, but in every situation, by prayer and petition, with thanksgiving, present your requests to God. And the peace of God, which transcends all understanding, will guard your hearts and your minds in Christ Jesus.' **Philippians 4:4–7**

Sometimes we can have the wrong outlook on life. We look for the negatives – for things to moan about, instead of the good that can come out of any situation where God is at work! To those of us that fall into this negativity trap, Paul (who wrote today's verses) says, 'Rejoice!' Why? Because God is near – what a brilliant promise!

Instead of worrying about the negatives, **we can bring our worries to God** – and leave them with Him. The word used for thanksgiving in the original Greek language of the New Testament comes from the word 'joy'. Thanks is expressing deep joy. So we could read that verse again as: 'with *joy* present your requests to God'. Talking with God is a happy experience. Prayer is something to get excited about. Be enthusiastic!

Be positive! God answers prayer, we can be sure of it – not only because we experience it ourselves but because the Bible says so!

What are the results of thanking God in every situation? Peace! The peace of God that protects us from getting wound up and bitter when the going gets tough.

So, it's not only what you say to God that's important but also the way you say it. As you speak with God, be grateful for all that He has done for you. When we are genuinely thankful it changes our outlook to see things as God does!

 Try and think about what your outlook on life has been this week. Has it mainly been negative? Have you felt moody and unthankful as a result? Or have you kept your eyes on God, praising and thanking Him in all situations? Have you felt His peace and joy as a result?

Father, please give me Your peace and help me to praise You in every sitiuation. Amen.

Hooked on worship

'It is good to praise the LORD and make music to your name, O Most High, proclaiming your love in the morning and your faithfulness at night, to the music of the ten-stringed lyre and the melody of the harp. For you make me glad by your deeds, LORD; I sing for joy at what your hands have done. How great are your works, LORD, how profound your thoughts! Senseless people do not know, fools do not understand, that though the wicked spring up like grass and all evildoers flourish, they will be destroyed for ever. But you, LORD, are for ever exalted.' **Psalm 92:1–8**

The Bible reading today encourages us to become a praise-aholic! This psalm was written to be sung on the Jewish day of rest, the Sabbath.

The Sabbath, the last day of the week, was a day of thanksgiving. People would meet to praise the Lord. It was a time to tune up the harp and ten-string lyre and sing in honour of God. Why? **Simply because it's good to praise the Lord!**

This song was also written to encourage people not to make praise a one day of the week event. Each morning they were to speak out and thank God for His love. Each evening they were to praise God for keeping His promises and caring for them. From dawn to dusk the Lord's name was to be praised.

For us that means from breakfast to bedtime we should remember God with great enthusiasm. **Praise isn't a once-a-week church-based activity, but a dynamic lifestyle.**

Engage

Do you need to spend more time worshipping God during the week? Why not put worship music on when you're in your room or in the car, and sing along? Try it! It's good for you and God deserves it!

Pray

Lord God, You are awesome and You deserve my praise. Please help me to make a habit of spending time with You every day. Amen.

A new song

'Sing to the LORD a new song, for he has done marvellous things … The LORD has made his salvation known and revealed his righteousness to the nations. He has remembered his love and his faithfulness to Israel; all the ends of the earth have seen the salvation of our God. Shout for joy to the LORD, all the earth, burst into jubilant song with music … Let the sea resound, and everything in it, the world, and all who live in it. Let the rivers clap their hands, let the mountains sing together for joy; let them sing before the LORD' **Psalm 98:1–4,7–9**

Great events in the Bible were often celebrated with a new song. What a great idea! **Who doesn't love hearing a brilliant new song for the first time?!**

And in today's verses we're given a reason for writing new praise songs: God is totally awesome.

Here's what is so incredible about God …

1. His power! God's right hand is a symbol of His power and authority. God's power is holy and He uses His authority over us for our good.

2. His salvation! He alone can save, forgive and make us right with Him.
3. His love! He never *ever* lets us down.

God is *colossally* awesome, so He should be *massively* celebrated! The whole of creation was made to give praise to God.

Engage

Write down the most brilliant thing God has done for you. Now, here's a challenge! Write a song about it! Try and write a chorus, which will be repeated, and a couple of verses if you can – you could even write a bridge if you're up for it (that's usually the bit when the song really builds and gets exciting)! If you play an instrument, could you write the music as well, and come up with a tune?! Sing it to God in private or maybe even to your friends at church!

Pray

Lord God, You've inspired so many amazing songs because You are totally wonderful! Please inspire me to write my own song to You. Amen.

A round of applause

'Clap your hands, all you nations; shout to God with cries of joy. For the LORD Most High is awesome, the great King over all the earth. He subdued nations under us, peoples under our feet. He chose our inheritance for us, the pride of Jacob, whom he loved. God has ascended amid shouts of joy, the LORD amid the sounding of trumpets. Sing praises to God, sing praises; sing praises to our King, sing praises. For God is the King of all the earth; sing to him a psalm of praise. God reigns over the nations; God is seated on his holy throne.' **Psalm 47:1–8**

People often put their hands together silently to pray. The Bible gives us another reason to put our hands together – to make some noise for the King!

There are many instances in the Bible when kings were applauded when they were crowned. People burst into spontaneous clapping and shouts of joy. So if that was right for kings, how much more should we applaud the King of kings!

Psalm 47 reminds us that God is an awesome King who reigns over all. He doesn't just deserve polite applause but **a thunderous standing ovation!**

And as you don't have to be musical to clap, everyone can join in.

Why do we give people applause? Well, we clap for people who perform well on the sports field or on stage – and no one performs better or wins more than our God! And applause is much more than clapping. It's an expression that we appreciate God in all that we do. And that means putting our hands together in practical ways to help other people, too.

The next time you're at church and everyone claps for God, why don't you join in, wholeheartedly? You could tell God right now why you think He is worth a massive round of applause.

Father, You are brilliant! I want to show You and others how amazing I think You are by praising You in anyway I can – even by simply clapping! Amen.

It's your weapon

'Let Israel rejoice in their Maker; let the people of Zion be glad in their King. Let them praise his name with dancing and make music to him with tambourine and harp. For the LORD takes delight in his people; he crowns the humble with victory. Let his faithful people rejoice in this honour and sing for joy on their beds. May the praise of God be in their mouths and a double-edged sword in their hands, to inflict vengeance on the nations and punishment on the peoples, to bind their kings with fetters, their nobles with shackles of iron, to carry out the sentence written against them – this is the glory of all his faithful people.'

Psalm 149:2–9

Here's a throwback to our chapter on the armour of God! Did you know our praise can be like a 'double-edged sword'? **Our praise is a weapon.** Against who? Well, as we learnt in that previous chapter, our fight is not against each other but against the devil and all evil.

When you're going through a tough time or if someone close to you is, it's hard to *feel like* worshipping. Even though you know God is not to blame, you just don't feel like singing or dancing and that is totally understandable, isn't it?

But if you push yourself to anyway, something pretty powerful happens. The devil, who is sitting there enjoying the fact that you're sad and in pain, gets delivered a huge blow when you raise your voice to God.

God gave us our voices for many reasons, let's not forget this one! **We can put the devil in his place.** He absolutely hates it when we praise God, so let's send him packing!

Engage

Read James 4:7. By praising God even in the tough times – even when we don't feel like it – we are resisting the devil. He wants us to keep quiet, to stop praising God. The next time you don't feel quite like singing in church, why don't you push yourself to? See what happens!

Pray

Dear Lord God, please help me to praise You, even when I'm not in the mood. You always deserve it! Amen.

Gifted or not

'Praise him with the sounding of the trumpet, praise him with the harp and lyre, praise him with tambourine and dancing, praise him with the strings and pipe, praise him with the clash of cymbals, praise him with resounding cymbals. Let everything that has breath praise the LORD.' **Psalm 150:3–6**

Today's verses have a brilliant message for those of us who are musical and for those who are not so much!

King David was a talented musician. He could have formed a band to celebrate his own greatness. Instead, he used his talents to draw people closer to God.

David raised up music groups to lead worship in the Temple. Musical Levites spent hours learning to play instruments (grade 8 tambourine!) and singing in choirs. Nothing but the best was offered to God.

But then we have some good news for those of us who are musically challenged! God says that *everything* that has breath can praise Him. The fact that you sound like a clashing cymbal rather than a melodious harp is no excuse to opt out, or for anyone else to put you down. To God, your worship is worship, whether you sing in tune or not.

So, we have advice for everyone – at both ends of the scale. If you are gifted: practise, practise, practise. There is nothing greater than using those God-given gifts and abilities to point people to Jesus. Practise your talents and use them for the glory of God! And if you're not musical: don't let that hold you back from raising your voice in worship – whether with others or on your own. God gave you breath, so use it to sing His praises in any way you can!

 Which piece of advice do you think you need to take to heart today? Could you encourage someone who is musical to practise their God-given gift? Could you encourage someone who tends to hold back from worshipping God to just go for it?!

Dear God, thank You for giving us all different gifts. Thank You for the gifts You have given me. I will praise Your name today, whether You gifted me with a musical ability or not. Amen.

Where?

'the woman said, "… Our ancestors worshipped on this mountain, but you Jews claim that the place where we must worship is in Jerusalem."

"Woman," Jesus replied, "believe me, a time is coming when you will worship the Father neither on this mountain nor in Jerusalem … Yet a time is coming and has now come when the true worshippers will worship the Father in the Spirit and in truth, for they are the kind of worshippers the Father seeks. God is spirit, and his worshippers must worship in the Spirit and in truth."'

John 4:19–21,23–24

I_w our reading today a woman with a strong viewpoint asks Jesus about the best place to worship.

The woman was a Samaritan, a mixed race of partly Jewish and partly foreign people. Jews despised Samaritans because they weren't pure-blooded Jews. Rather than worship at the Temple in Jerusalem, the Samaritans built their own temple on Mount Gerizim. Although the building was destroyed in 128 BC, the Samaritans still worshipped on the mountain top. Years later the Jews and Samaritans (who both followed God's laws) were still arguing over the best place to worship.

Notice that Jesus didn't get pulled into the argument about their mountain-top experiences. Instead He pointed out that it is not *where* you worship but *how* you worship that makes the difference. Worship must be true! Worship must be led by the Holy Spirit! That's the worship God wants!

People still argue over worship, preferring one church's style to another. We need to realise that **we can worship God** *anywhere.* The challenge is to be full of the Holy Spirit so that we don't put on an act or follow a routine.

 It's so easy to fall into the weekly routine of going to church on Sunday, singing the songs, and then for the rest of the week not actually living out the words we sang about. The next time you're at church, why don't you ask God to let some words in a song stand out to you? Then really try to apply them to your daily life for the rest of the week. That's true worship – when our words follow us and become actions!

Lord God, please help me to worship You in a real way today, no matter where I am. Amen.

Detox

'live by the Spirit, and you will not gratify the desires of the flesh. For the flesh desires what is contrary to the Spirit, and the Spirit what is contrary to the flesh … But if you are led by the Spirit, you are not under the law. The acts of the flesh are obvious: sexual immorality, impurity and debauchery; idolatry and witchcraft; hatred, discord, jealousy, fits of rage, selfish ambition, dissensions, factions and envy; drunkenness … the fruit of the Spirit is love, joy, peace, forbearance, kindness, goodness, faithfulness, gentleness and self-control. Against such things there is no law. Those who belong to Christ Jesus have crucified the flesh with its passions and desires. Since we live by the Spirit, let us keep in step with the Spirit.' **Galatians 5:16–25**

Have you ever heard of a detox diet? It's the idea that you can flush out all the 'bad' stuff – the toxins – in the body (whatever they are!) by eating and drinking the 'right' stuff. Well, today, let's think about how we can clear out all the 'bad stuff' that can grow in our hearts. These things can hinder our worship of God and our relationship with Him. So it's really important we understand what these things can be and how we get rid of them!

To answer what they are, we can find them in verses 19–21 of today's reading. These 'acts of the flesh' include things like greed, hatred, jealousy, anger, selfish ambitions. If we allow these things to take root and grow in our hearts by not sorting them out quickly, they can squash our desire to worship God.

So, let's sort it out! How? With the Holy Spirit's help! By welcoming the Holy Spirit in we are allowing Him to **replace all these selfish attitudes with His 'fruit':** things like peace, kindness, joy and self-control! What a detox!

This isn't an instant process; it takes time, but more and more the Holy Spirit will help you **so that you can be running over with praise.**

Engage

Have a think about your thoughts and actions recently. Do you think they suggest some selfish attitudes may be taking root in your heart? Don't fear! Ask the Holy Spirit to fill you up right now!

Pray

Lord, I don't want to be held back from giving You my true worship and adoration. Please forgive any selfishness in my heart and fill me with the Holy Spirit. Amen.

Generous worship

'Give, and it will be given to you. A good measure, pressed down, shaken together and running over, will be poured into your lap. For with the measure you use, it will be measured to you.' **Luke 6:38**

*O*n the packaging of many cereals there is the warning that, as the contents settle, the volume may shrink. This is to stop people opening their cornflakes and thinking they've been robbed!

In Bible times, generous traders would fill a sack with grain then press the contents down and refill it to the top.

So today we're talking about being generous worshippers! God has a principle that the more we give, the more we receive. When we make a sacrifice of praise, God has His own ways of seeing that we benefit. He appreciates what we do for Him and shows it. Often, as we open out in praise to God, He gives us great joy and encouragement.

Like a generous trader, God wants to fill us with His Spirit, shake us up and refill us to overflowing. **We can then be free to share His generosity with the world around us.**

Think about it. Reluctant giving doesn't help anyone. We don't benefit if we praise God because we have to or because it is the done thing, and God can see right through us when we put on an act of worshipping rather than really praising Him in our hearts. Have you ever been complimented by someone but it didn't feel, or blatantly wasn't, genuine? It can be hurtful, can't it?!

When we express God's greatness in a real way we will find great satisfaction in giving praise to Him. Don't short-change God, because He always gives more than we deserve!

Engage

Praise is something we give to God but there are many ways to give. Some people give out of duty, some give grudgingly, some give generously. How will you give to God this week?

Pray

Lord, You deserve all my praise. Help me give it joyfully today! Amen.

Praise makes a way

'The crowd joined in the attack against Paul and Silas, and the magistrates ordered them to be stripped and beaten with rods. After they had been severely flogged, they were thrown into prison, and the jailer was commanded to guard them carefully … he put them in the inner cell and fastened their feet in the stocks. About midnight Paul and Silas were praying and singing hymns to God, and the other prisoners were listening to them. Suddenly there was such a violent earthquake that the foundations of the prison were shaken. At once all the prison doors flew open, and everyone's chains came loose.' **Acts 16:22–26**

Having been set upon by a mob and then beaten unmercifully across their bare backs with whips, Paul and Silas had every reason to feel sorry for themselves. To make matters worse they were stretched out on their backs on the filthy prison floor, their hands and feet held firmly in stocks.

In all their suffering, Paul and Silas were never once abusive to their captors. Nor did they feel angry towards

God for letting this happen. Instead they prayed aloud in front of the other prisoners and sang songs of praise. **As the praise went up, God's power came down.** The whole prison shook, their chains came loose and their door to freedom opened.

The jailer, who had been moved by the praise and the miracle, asked the most important question anyone can ask: 'What must I do to be saved?' Paul and Silas, who could easily have been more interested in doing a runner, stayed around to help the jailer with the words, 'Believe on the Lord Jesus and you will be saved!' Praise not only opened the prison but also a continent. The jailer was the first man in Europe to become a Christian!

When things get tough, do you get low on self-pity or high on praise? Praising God resulted in freedom, in bringing others to Jesus and in new opportunities for Paul and Silas.

God, thank You that there is power in praise – that You open doors and make a way for me when it first seemed impossible, no matter what situation it might be. Amen.

Sisterhood

'There was also a prophet, Anna … She was very old; she had lived with her husband seven years after her marriage, and then was a widow until she was eighty-four. She never left the temple but worshipped night and day, fasting and praying. Coming up to them at that very moment, she gave thanks to God and spoke about the child to all who were looking forward to the redemption of Jerusalem.' **Luke 2:36–38**

Celebrities aside, who do you look up to? Is there a woman at church or a family member who you think is really inspirational? And what is it about them that makes you feel this way? Are they kind and generous, talented in some way or really good at giving advice?

The girls and women around us were put there for a reason, did you know that? It was God's idea for us to have each other: to share life with, to challenge and strengthen each other; to learn from each other!

In this last chapter, we are going to find out about some of the women in the Bible. They each have something to teach us, through their highs and lows, successes and mistakes; flaws and strengths. And we start today with Anna.

For the majority of Anna's life she was a widow. She would have known what it really meant to be lonely. **But what an inspiration she was!** She never left the Temple. Day *and night* she worshipped, fasted and prayed. She wanted to be in God's presence all the time. She wanted to put Him first. And God blessed her greatly. That child she laid her eyes on was Jesus Himself. She knew He was her Lord and Saviour straightaway – she knew God so well.

 We can have so much going on in our lives that it distracts us from really getting to know God. Anna pursued God more than anything else. Have a think about this: if God spoke to you right now, do you think you know Him well enough to recognise Him? What could you perhaps cut down on (watching TV, Facebook etc) that would give you more time to spend with God?

Father, thank You for putting other women of God around me who I can learn so much from. Help me to remember Anna. I pray I will follow her example and put You first in my life. Amen.

Queen Esther

'Mordecai had a cousin named Hadassah, whom he had brought up because she had neither father nor mother. This young woman, who was also known as Esther, had a lovely figure and was beautiful ... When the king's order and edict had been proclaimed, many young women were brought to the citadel of Susa and put under the care of Hegai. Esther also was taken to the king's palace ... Esther had not revealed her nationality and family background, because Mordecai had forbidden her to do so.' **Esther 2:7–8,10**

Esther was not only an orphan but also a Jew, which meant she didn't seem to have much going for her. But God had chosen her with a plan in mind that would turn her life around – and the lives of many others.

The king wanted a new wife and so he threw a sort of beauty contest to find one. Everywhere Esther went she found favour with people, meaning they liked her, treated her well and wanted the best for her. And that included the king. He fell for her instantly.

So this girl went from rags to riches, from orphan to queen, just like that! She knew what it was like to have nothing and *be* nothing but now she was catapulted into a position of great power. As her life played out as queen, it became obvious she was where she was for a reason – a very important one indeed! The king's right-hand man, Haman, despised Jews and he managed to set up a law that meant they could all be wiped out. Little did Haman know, he had set up a law to kill his own queen. It was time for Esther to reveal who she was.

So she went to the king, even though it could very well have meant her death (as she was breaking royal protocol) but her obedience and courage paid off. Through her, God saved the Jews from certain death.

Despite her massive change of circumstances, **Esther remained the same faithful girl through it all.** Perhaps that's why God chose her for the job! He saw her heart and knew she would follow Him wherever He led her.

Engage

If your circumstances changed as dramatically as Esther's, do you think you'd stay the same girl? Would you be obedient to God through it all?

Pray

Lord God, please guide and keep me safe like You did Esther. I want to follow wherever You lead. Amen.

The very first woman

'God commanded the man, "You are free to eat from any tree in the garden; but you must not eat from the tree of the knowledge of good and evil, for when you eat from it you will certainly die." … When the woman saw that the fruit of the tree was good for food and pleasing to the eye, and also desirable for gaining wisdom, she took some and ate it. She also gave some to her husband, who was with her, and he ate it … Then the man and his wife heard the sound of the LORD God as he was walking in the garden in the cool of the day, and they hid … Then the LORD God said to the woman, "What is this you have done?"

The woman said, "The snake deceived me, and I ate."' **Genesis 2:16–17; 3:6,8,13**

Esther was known for her brilliant obedience – Eve … not so much! Let's see what advice we can gain from the first woman who ever walked the earth …

When God created Adam and Eve, it showed us just how much He cares about relationships. There they lived in paradise, together with God. They had everything they could ever want or need. God gave them one rule – to not eat from a certain tree – but other than that, God pretty much said, 'Enjoy!'

Then along came the snake (the devil), and with him came temptation. Master of lies, the devil persuaded Eve to disobey God and, standing with her, Adam joined in. This is what is known as 'the Fall' – when humankind (as Adam and Eve represented us all) turned from God and went their own way.

It can be quite hard to relate to Eve. After all, we don't know that much about her. But what we can relate to is the fact that **we face the same challenge of obedience every day.** We know God's rules and guidance, just as Eve knew, and we are tempted to turn from God by the very same devil. With Eve, we can learn from her mistake and not do the same.

Engage   **What good did hiding from God do for Adam and Eve? Are you tempted to do the same when you mess up?**

Pray

Father God, thank You that with You I have the strength to resist the devil. I want to follow You, always. Amen.

A widow's faith

'The wife of a man … cried out to Elisha, "Your servant my husband is dead … now his creditor is coming to take my two boys as his slaves." Elisha replied to her, "… Tell me, what do you have in your house?" … she said, "… a small jar of olive oil." Elisha said, "Go round and ask all your neighbours for empty jars. Don't ask for just a few. Then go inside and shut the door behind you and your sons. Pour oil into all the jars, and as each is filled, put it to one side." She left him and shut the door behind her and her sons. They brought the jars to her and she kept pouring. When all the jars were full … the oil stopped flowing. She went and told the man of God, and he said, "Go, sell the oil and pay your debts. You and your sons can live on what is left."' **2 Kings 4:1–7**

Try to put yourself in this woman's shoes. She had lost her husband, she was bankrupt and now her sons were being threatened with slavery. This was extreme poverty. Yet she knew a man of God and she still had a little bit of faith left.

This man, Elisha, gave her some pretty odd instructions and although she had no idea how God was going to sort out her financial problems, she did as he told her.

The widow had to bury her pride and be humble. It couldn't have been easy explaining to her neighbours why she wanted to borrow their jars. She was willing to give the little oil she had because **she believed that God was going to work a miracle.**

God multiplied her small offering and she filled jar after jar with oil! This would pay her debts and save her sons from slavery!

Engage

The Bible says that 'without faith it is impossible to please God' (Heb. 11:6). When we face seemingly hard or impossible situations, can we trust and obey God as much as that woman did?

Pray

Lord, You have proved, time and time again, that You are completely faithful and trustworthy. You will always provide for me. Help my faith stand against any test I may face. Amen.

When Sarah laughed

'The LORD appeared to Abraham … Abraham looked up and saw three men standing nearby. When he saw them, he hurried from the entrance of his tent to meet them and bowed low to the ground … "Where is your wife Sarah?" they asked him. "There, in the tent," he said. Then one of them said, "I will surely return to you about this time next year, and Sarah your wife will have a son."

Now Sarah was listening … [she] laughed to herself as she thought, "After I am worn out and my lord is old, will I now have this pleasure?"

Then the LORD said to Abraham, "Why did Sarah laugh and say, 'Will I really have a child, now that I am old?' Is anything too hard for the LORD? I will return to you at the appointed time next year, and Sarah will have a son."' **Genesis 18:1–2,9–14**

Sarah was 90 years old, so you can understand why she laughed at the idea of becoming pregnant this late in life! God had promised her and Abraham that they would have children. Had He changed His mind?

We can imagine that beneath this reaction, Sarah was holding onto a lot of hurt. She had waited years to become pregnant and her hopes had been continuously raised and dashed. She had also allowed Abraham to have a baby with one of their servants, to give Abraham an heir, and that caused lots of family rows.

But God heard Sarah and He answered her.

A year later Sarah was laughing again (Gen. 21:1–6). This time it wasn't a cynical scoff but an outburst of joy as she held her new-born son Isaac. God had healed her hurt and taken away past doubts.

Fears, failures and hurts can cause us to lose faith in ourselves, others and even God. But **God will never break a promise.** He will never let us down.

Are any hurts from the past hindering your faith in God? Talk to another Christian about it, maybe a leader at your church, and ask them to pray for you.

Dear God, You are bigger than my doubts, failures or hurts. Please help me to let these things go and trust You instead. Amen.

Face whatever, together

'At that time Mary got ready and hurried to a town in the hill country of Judea, where she entered Zechariah's home and greeted Elizabeth. When Elizabeth heard Mary's greeting, the baby leaped in her womb, and Elizabeth was filled with the Holy Spirit. In a loud voice she exclaimed: "Blessed are you among women, and blessed is the child you will bear! But why am I so favoured, that the mother of my Lord should come to me? As soon as the sound of your greeting reached my ears, the baby in my womb leaped for joy. Blessed is she who has believed that the Lord would fulfil his promises to her!" … Mary stayed with Elizabeth for about three months and then returned home.'

Luke 1:39–45,56

Mary had recently found out that she was pregnant with the Son of God. Now the first part of this fact was scary enough – pregnant! Can you imagine all the fears and worries rushing through her head at that moment? And the *Son of God*? Amazing, yes, but how was she meant to explain this to others? How would God want her to raise Him?!

Mary did what many of us would do when facing something new, overwhelming or downright terrifying – **she went to see a friend.** And not only that, she went to see a friend who was experiencing a similar thing! Elizabeth was also pregnant. They could be open and chat about everything, they could understand and support each other.

These young women were carrying Jesus and John the Baptist. John made a way for Jesus and His ministry, and Jesus, well, He did *everything* for us! Little did Mary and Elizabeth know at the time!

So when you're facing something new or scary, don't ever face it alone. God can use all situations to bring about His good plans, we just have to be willing!

Are you tempted to say 'no' to any opportunities from God at the moment? Before you do, why don't you talk to someone about it? Could you find someone at church who has gone through it themselves?

Lord, please help me to be a supportive friend and to go to others when I need support myself. Amen.

When's my turn?

'There was a certain man … whose name was Elkanah … He had two wives; one was called Hannah and the other Peninnah. Peninnah had children, but Hannah had none … Because the LORD had closed Hannah's womb, her rival kept provoking her in order to irritate her. This went on year after year. Whenever Hannah went up to the house of the LORD, her rival provoked her till she wept and would not eat.' **1 Samuel 1:1–2,6–7**

As we go through life, we can experience big things like getting a boyfriend, graduating from university, getting a job, getting engaged, buying a house, becoming pregnant, and so on!

These things are great! *But* it's important to remember that **these things don't always happen at the same time for us and our friends.** And sometimes it can create a bit of tension or underlying sadness when some are experiencing these things while others are still waiting for 'their turn'. It can feel a little bit like being left behind – not nice! Have you ever felt like this?

Hannah felt this pain. She desperately wanted a baby but it seemed as though it would never be 'her turn'.

And instead of being a friend, Penninah was completely insensitive, rubbing in the fact that she had children and Hannah didn't.

This does happen. We do experience these big life changes at different times to our friends, but through it all friendship can last. When we're waiting for something, or our friends are, let's be open and honest with each other, praying for each other and being sensitive to each other's feelings.

God gave Hannah her heart's desire (in His timing) and He promises to do the same for us.

Engage If you are experiencing this feeling of being left behind, remember that almost everyone has felt this way at some point in their lives! Don't feel pressured to rush your life; keep waiting patiently and trust that God is in control. If you're not feeling this way, think about whether any of your friends might be at the moment, and tell them that you're there for them if they ever want to talk about it.

Pray

Lord, You see the bigger picture of my life. If I ever have to wait longer than I'd like to, please help me to have patience. I trust You. Amen.

There first

'Many women were there … They had followed Jesus from Galilee to care for his needs … After the Sabbath, at dawn on the first day of the week, Mary Magdalene and the other Mary went to look at the tomb. There was a violent earthquake, for an angel of the Lord came down from heaven … The angel said to the women, "Do not be afraid, for I know that you are looking for Jesus, who was crucified. He is not here; he has risen … go quickly and tell his disciples …" So the women hurried away from the tomb, afraid yet filled with joy, and ran to tell his disciples. Suddenly Jesus met them. "Greetings," he said. They came to him, clasped his feet and worshipped him.'

Matthew 27:55; 28:1–2,5–9

These women were the first to witness the resurrected Jesus. They were the first to see that Jesus had defeated death – that He really was the Son of God, come to save the world! **What a privilege!** And why was it them? What made them so special? Well, it was simply down to the fact that they were there first!

They cared so much about Jesus. While He lived, they looked after Him and while He was dead, they made it their first priority to go and care for His body. They understood Jesus' teaching about serving others and they were brilliant examples of how we should live our lives.

And their devotion to Jesus was rewarded! They were also the first to go and spread the good news of Jesus to others.

How excited do you get when you hear about a new show on TV, or when you get a brilliant new gadget or beauty product? You just want to tell *everyone* about it, don't you? Our excitement about Jesus should be a billion times that much! We should be absolutely bursting with the good news!

 Sometimes this enthusiasm dies or was never that big to begin with. Are you enthusiastic about Jesus? If not, don't be hard on yourself! The Holy Spirit gives us this passion! If you want it, ask for it now!

Holy Spirit, I don't want to miss an opportunity to experience the presence of God or to tell others the good news. Please fill me with excitement and eagerness now. Amen.

Come back later

'As Jesus and his disciples were on their way, he came to a village where a woman named Martha opened her home to him. She had a sister called Mary, who sat at the Lord's feet listening to what he said. But Martha was distracted by all the preparations that had to be made. She came to him and asked, "Lord, don't you care that my sister has left me to do the work by myself? Tell her to help me!" "Martha, Martha," the Lord answered, "you are worried and upset about many things, but few things are needed – or indeed only one. Mary has chosen what is better, and it will not be taken away from her."' **Luke 10:38–42**

Have you ever been too busy to spend time with your friends? 'Sorry, I can't come out right now!' It's fine now and then – totally understandable – but if we're too busy all the time, it affects our friendship. A crucial part of what makes us friends is spending time with each other and it's no different when it comes to our relationship with God.

Martha had invited Jesus and His friends into her home. She wanted them to be comfortable, to have food and be in a clean and tidy environment. **There was a lot to do!** You can understand why she got a little annoyed at Mary for just sitting there 'doing nothing'.

Jesus responded lovingly yet honestly to Martha. Mary wasn't simply doing nothing. Like the women we read about in the last reading, Mary was putting Jesus first. She didn't want to take her eyes of Him or miss a single moment of spending time with Him.

And Jesus wanted Martha to realise that putting Him first is the most important thing.

Have a think about how you've spent your week so far. Have you been too busy to spend time with Jesus? What's getting in the way and is it really that important?

Lord Jesus, I don't want to miss out on spending time with You. Please help me see when I'm getting too busy and show me the things that aren't important so I can replace them with You. Amen.

Where you go, I go

'Elimelek, Naomi's husband, died, and she was left with her two sons. They married Moabite women, one named Orpah and the other Ruth. After they had lived there about ten years, both Mahlon and Kilion also died, and Naomi was left without her two sons and her husband … Naomi said to her two daughters-in-law, "Go back, each of you, to your mother's home … May the LORD grant that each of you will find rest in the home of another husband.".… Orpah kissed her mother-in-law goodbye, but Ruth clung to her … "Don't urge me to leave you … Where you go I will go, and where you stay I will stay. Your people will be my people and your God my God …" When Naomi realised that Ruth was determined to go with her, she stopped urging her. So the two women went on until they came to Bethlehem.' **Ruth 1:3–5,8–9,14,16,18–19**

Many young women in Ruth's situation would have ditched their mother-in-law. It sounds harsh, but they were both now widows and in those days that meant living an impoverished life. As she was still young, Ruth could easily remarry in her hometown. There was still 'hope for her'.

However, instead of remaining in Moab, her homeland, **Ruth chose to live with Naomi and support her.** Why was she giving up her chances of getting remarried? Why was she being so loyal to Naomi? Well, Ruth had decided that Naomi's God would be her God and she knew God's way wasn't to ditch someone in need.

Ruth worked doubly hard to support Naomi. And God has His own way of rewarding those who put Him first. Her new job brought her to meet Boaz, a good man who would eventually marry her! And God blessed Ruth and Boaz with a son (and Naomi with a grandson!). Little did they know that they would be the great-grandparents of King David! What's more, they were in the family line of Jesus Himself!

 Engage   **Sometimes we miss what God has for us because we're chasing our own agenda. But when we stay loyal to God, going where He wants us to, we will get the best out of life (with lots of great surprises along the way)!**

Pray

Lord, I want to be like Ruth and stay loyal to You. Wherever You go, I go. Amen.

Fight!

'Therefore, my brothers and sisters, you whom I love and long for, my joy and crown, stand firm in the Lord in this way, dear friends! I plead with Euodia and I plead with Syntyche to be of the same mind in the Lord. Yes, and I ask you, my true companion, help these women since they have contended at my side in the cause of the gospel, along with Clement and the rest of my co-workers, whose names are in the book of life.'

Philippians 4:1–3

When Euodia and Syntyche fell out it caused all kinds of tensions and strife in the church. And the disagreements between them grew. They no longer used their feet to go and tell others about Jesus, they started to trample on each other's feelings instead.

We've all been in silly arguments that get out of control. It goes something like this: we fall out, we get others to take 'our side', then we find out what 'their side' has been saying about us and feel angry and hurt, so then we plan ways to get back at them and so on …

Paul told the two women to stop fighting each other and team up to tell others about Jesus – just as they had done in the past. **We need to save our energy to fight the right things.** As we read about in the first chapter of this book, we are not in a fight with each other; we are in a fight when it comes to good and evil. There are so many people who do not yet know Jesus, whose lives would be completely changed if we listened to God and stepped out to help them find God for themselves.

God was nearby waiting to help those women sort things out (see Phil. 4:5). Instead of getting worried or wound up, God wants us to off-load our concerns on Him. He can deal with our negative thoughts and help us live at peace with Him, ourselves and others.

Engage **Have you been in an argument recently? Why don't you apologise and make peace with that person? Ask God to give you the humility and courage to do so.**

Pray

Lord, I give all my concerns over to You. When I don't see eye-to-eye with another Christian, please help us both come to a peaceful compromise. Amen.

What she's known for

'there was a disciple named Tabitha (in Greek her name is Dorcas); she was always doing good and helping the poor. About that time she became ill and died … Peter … arrived … All the widows stood round him, crying and showing him the robes and other clothing that Dorcas had made while she was still with them. Peter … prayed. Turning towards the dead woman, he said, "Tabitha, get up." She opened her eyes, and seeing Peter she sat up. He took her by the hand and helped her to her feet. Then he called for the believers, especially the widows, and presented her to them alive … many people believed in the Lord.'

Acts 9:36–42

Today we meet Dorcas, a woman who shone a light for Jesus in a dark place. The port town Joppa had suffered much grief over the years. Many of the Jewish sailors had been lost at sea and so the town was full of impoverished widows and orphans.

Dorcas was known there for her kindness. She made clothes to give to the poor, she comforted widows and cared for orphans. She was loved by many. So when the news came that Dorcas had died, the town was devastated at the loss of this generous woman.

Peter was nearby in Lydda, so two Christians shot off to get him. The burial was delayed until Peter arrived. Peter went into the room where her body lay, then a few minutes later returned with Dorcas – alive and well!

It turns out he'd got on his knees, prayed in the name of Jesus, then told her to get up – and she did! News spread like wildfire and the port came to a standstill as people crowded to see Dorcas and hear Peter tell them about the power of Jesus. Many sailors, traders and businessmen, along with their families, became Christians.

Dorcas made a way into people's hearts through her kindness. No doubt people asked why she was so generous and she told them about Jesus. Kindness often paves the way!

What do you think you're 'known for'? Being a Christian is more than just what we say, it's how we behave and what we do.

Jesus, thank You for the power of kindness and generosity. Please help me to show these qualities more today. Amen.

Right place at the right time

'she became pregnant and gave birth to a son ... when she could hide him no longer, she got a papyrus basket … placed the child in it and put it among the reeds along the bank of the Nile. His sister stood at a distance to see what would happen to him. Then Pharaoh's daughter went down to the Nile to bathe ... She saw the basket … She opened it and saw the baby ... she felt sorry for him. "This is one of the Hebrew babies," she said. Then his sister asked Pharaoh's daughter, "Shall I go and get one of the Hebrew women to nurse the baby for you?"

"Yes, go," she answered ... When the child grew older, she took him to Pharaoh's daughter and he became her son. She named him Moses, saying, "I drew him out of the water."' **Exodus 2:2–8,10**

A new pharaoh had come to power in Egypt and he was worried that there were too many Israelites (God's people) in the country. He believed they would turn on him and join his enemies. He ordered his slave masters to oppress them and work them ruthlessly.

Worse still, he gave this order: 'Every Hebrew boy that is born you must throw into the Nile, but let every girl live' (Exod. 1:22).

And this is how Moses' story begins. He was one of those Hebrew baby boys. But God placed some people in his life who would keep him safe. We read today of how his mother hid him and his sister, Miriam, watched over him.

Then along came the pharaoh's daughter. **Miriam was in the right place at the right time** because she was able to witness her brother being saved. The pharaoh's daughter found Moses. She recognised that he was Hebrew and she knew what that meant. But she took pity on him and made a decision, along with Miriam, that would save his life.

Because of them, Moses lived, and he went on to lead the Israelites out of Egypt and their oppression. When we go where God wants us to, we will be in the right place for Him to use us for extraordinary things!

Engage   **Could you look out for someone today to be kind to or help in some way?**

Pray

Lord, please lead me to be where You want me today, doing the things You want me to do. Amen.

Material girl

'The two angels arrived at Sodom in the evening, and Lot was sitting in the gateway of the city ... The two men said to Lot, "Do you have anyone else here – sons-in-law, sons or daughters, or anyone else in the city who belongs to you? Get them out of here, because we are going to destroy this place. The outcry to the LORD against its people is so great that he has sent us to destroy it … Flee for your lives! Don't look back …" Then the LORD rained down burning sulphur on Sodom and Gomorrah … destroying all those living in the cities – and also the vegetation in the land. But Lot's wife looked back, and she became a pillar of salt.' **Genesis 19:1,12–13,17,24–26**

She's simply known as Lot's wife. She and Lot had set out with Abraham wanting to follow God but they'd compromised and opted for their get-rich-quick lifestyle. Lot set up a business in Sodom, a city full of sin and wrong living. We all have the choice of serving God or money and they had chosen money.

Now Sodom had become such a hotbed of evil that God decided to wipe it out.

Still looking out for Lot, God sent two angels to give him a second chance. However, when the angels warned them to get out of the city fast – without stopping or looking back – Lot's wife didn't take God seriously. She hesitated to leave all that she loved. Money, glamour, luxury – she wanted it all but she lost it all – along with her life.

This is a dramatic story but its lesson still applies to us today. If we put material things – or anything else for that matter – above God, we'll eventually lose out massively. But **if we put God first, we gain everything that really matters.**

 Jesus talked about this too. Read Luke 17:28–33. Have a think about what you're putting first in your heart. It's easy to slip into loving material things when we're surrounded by so many adverts. But ask Jesus for help in this and He will be all you need.

Lord Jesus, I don't want to be like Lot's wife and lose sight of what's really important. Please help me to put You first. Amen.

Lead the way

'Deborah, a prophet … was leading Israel at that time. She held court under the Palm of Deborah … and the Israelites went up to her to have their disputes decided. She sent for Barak … and said to him, "The LORD … commands you: 'Go, take with you ten thousand men … and lead them up to Mount Tabor. I will lead Sisera … and his troops … and give him into your hands.'" Barak said to her, "If you go with me, I will go; but if you don't go with me, I won't go."

"Certainly I will go with you," said Deborah. "But because of the course you are taking, the honour will not be yours, for the LORD will deliver Sisera into the hands of a woman." So Deborah went with Barak' **Judges 4:4–9**

Deborah was the top decision-maker in the land. She loved God and it showed. People visited her to get guidance and help in making decisions. And she humbly sorted out disputes. **She was highly respected.**

She didn't shy away from telling people to trust God. It wasn't because she was bossy, it was simply that she knew God could help them. She led by quiet example.

And when Barak hesitated to gather an army, Deborah got ready for battle herself to give him support.

She told the troops that God had promised them victory. Attacking the advanced army of 900 chariots with wooden farming implements required some serious faith. But Deborah had the power of prayer. God stormed in to flood the valley and ground the chariots. The Israelites were able to attack their enemies and gain freedom.

What a woman! Her example inspires us not to be scared to stand up for what we know is right. With God on our side, we'll have all the wisdom, power and courage we'll need!

 People respect and follow those who stand up for what they believe in. Have you noticed something that needs God's help to sort it out? Is there a bully at school or even some wrong things going on in your friendship group at church? Don't fight anything on your own. Take Deborah's advice and talk to God about it right now.

Dear God, I want to be brave like Deborah. No matter what I face today I know You are by my side. Thank You. Amen.

Sisters

'Be completely humble and gentle; be patient, bearing with one another in love. Make every effort to keep the unity of the Spirit through the bond of peace. There is one body and one Spirit, just as you were called to one hope when you were called; one Lord, one faith, one baptism; one God and Father of all, who is over all and through all and in all.' **Ephesians 4:2–6**

God didn't want us to ever feel alone (remember Adam and Eve?), that's why He gave us each other! We are all daughters of God – sisters! We not only lead people to Jesus individually but we can do it together. God made us to be united as we read in today's verses.

Relationships in the world can be pretty selfish. People only give love when they receive it or show kindness when they believe it's 'deserved'. This is not God's way; He shows love unconditionally.

When people see the way we relate to each other, like God really meant us to, they will notice the difference. When we stop gossip in its tracks, when we freely forgive those who have hurt us, when we are generous, when we show we understand – people will want to know what makes us this way. And we can answer: Jesus. And some people will want to be a part of it too!

So let's pray and praise God together. Let's learn together. **Let's be brave together.**

The secret of unity – like the world has never seen it – is God! God's love binds us together. It shows us the good in each of us so we can focus on those qualities. It works in all of us to make us more like Jesus. So let's put God first in everything and not forget each other.

Engage

Write this down somewhere you will see it every day (and why not make it your prayer?) ...
I want to be obedient like Esther, kind to others like Dorcas, patient like Hannah, focused on God like Mary, guided by God like Miriam and brave like Deborah. And finally, I want to never forget the importance of spending time with others, like Mary and Elizabeth.

Pray

Father God, please help me play my part in Your family. Help me love others unconditionally like You do. Strengthen us as we work together. Amen.

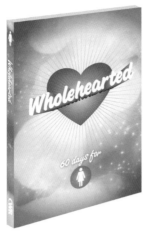

Wholehearted

Explore how we can rise
up to any challenge, know
Jesus better and hear some
wise words for our lives!
ISBN: 978-1-78259-353-9

Live Love Dream

From self-image to sharing
the gospel with friends,
discover what the Bible has
to say, and what good things
God has in store for you!
ISBN: 978-1-78259-100-9

For prices and to order, visit **www.cwr.org.uk/youth**

Also available online or from Christian bookshops.

YP's daily Bible reading notes

Read a bit of the Bible every day, explore lots of stuff about you and God, while cracking puzzles and playing quizzes along the way!

Available as individual issues (each issue covers two months) or annual subscription.

For prices and to order, visit **www.cwr.org.uk/youth**

Also available online or from Christian bookshops.

Guide to Knowing God

How can we know and understand God? What do
followers of Jesus really believe, and why? Explore
these questions and more, and see how what you
believe about God really does affect your life.
ISBN: 978-1-78259-182-5

For price and to order, visit **www.cwr.org.uk/youth**

Also available online or from Christian bookshops